Adult Eyes Only

23 Unique Pages

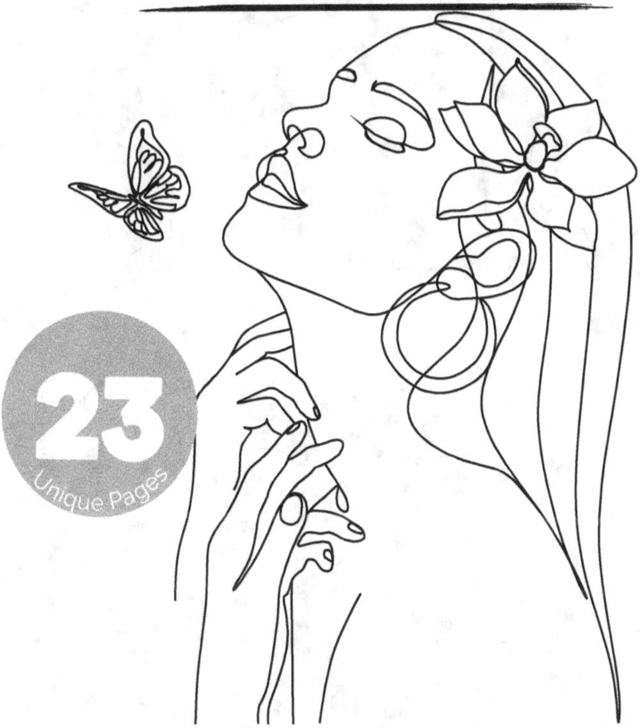

Coloring Book to Get You in the Mood

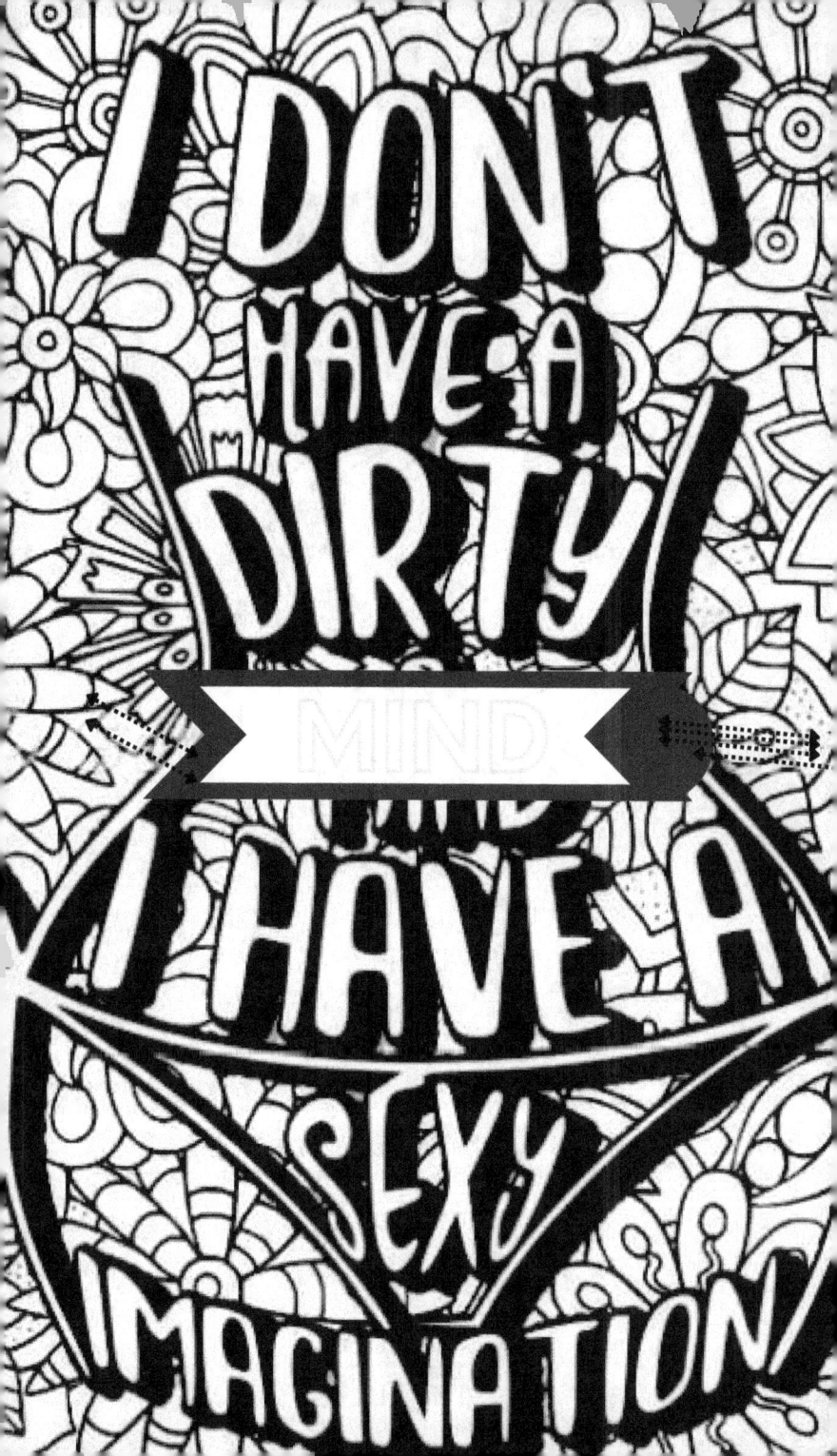

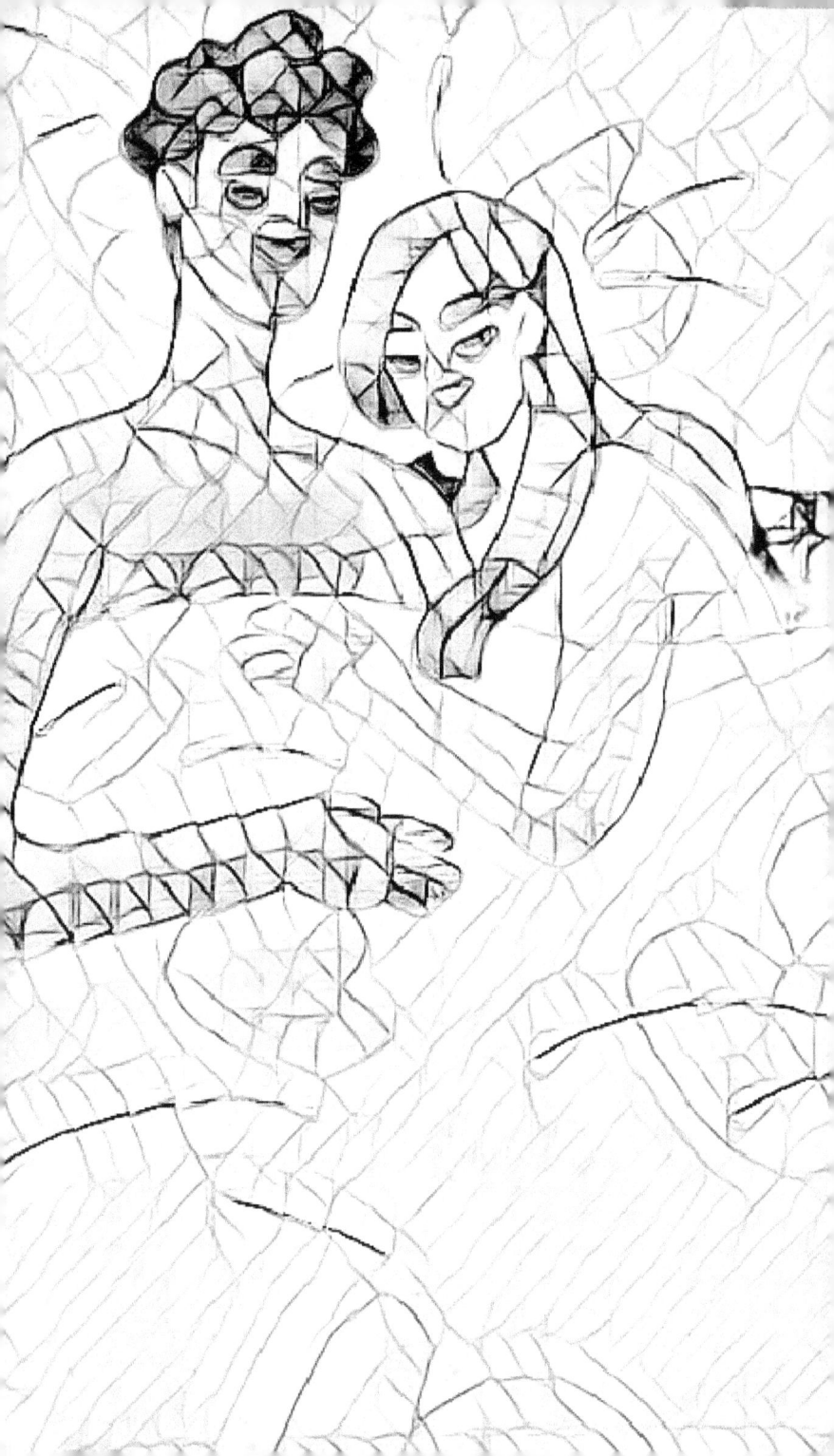

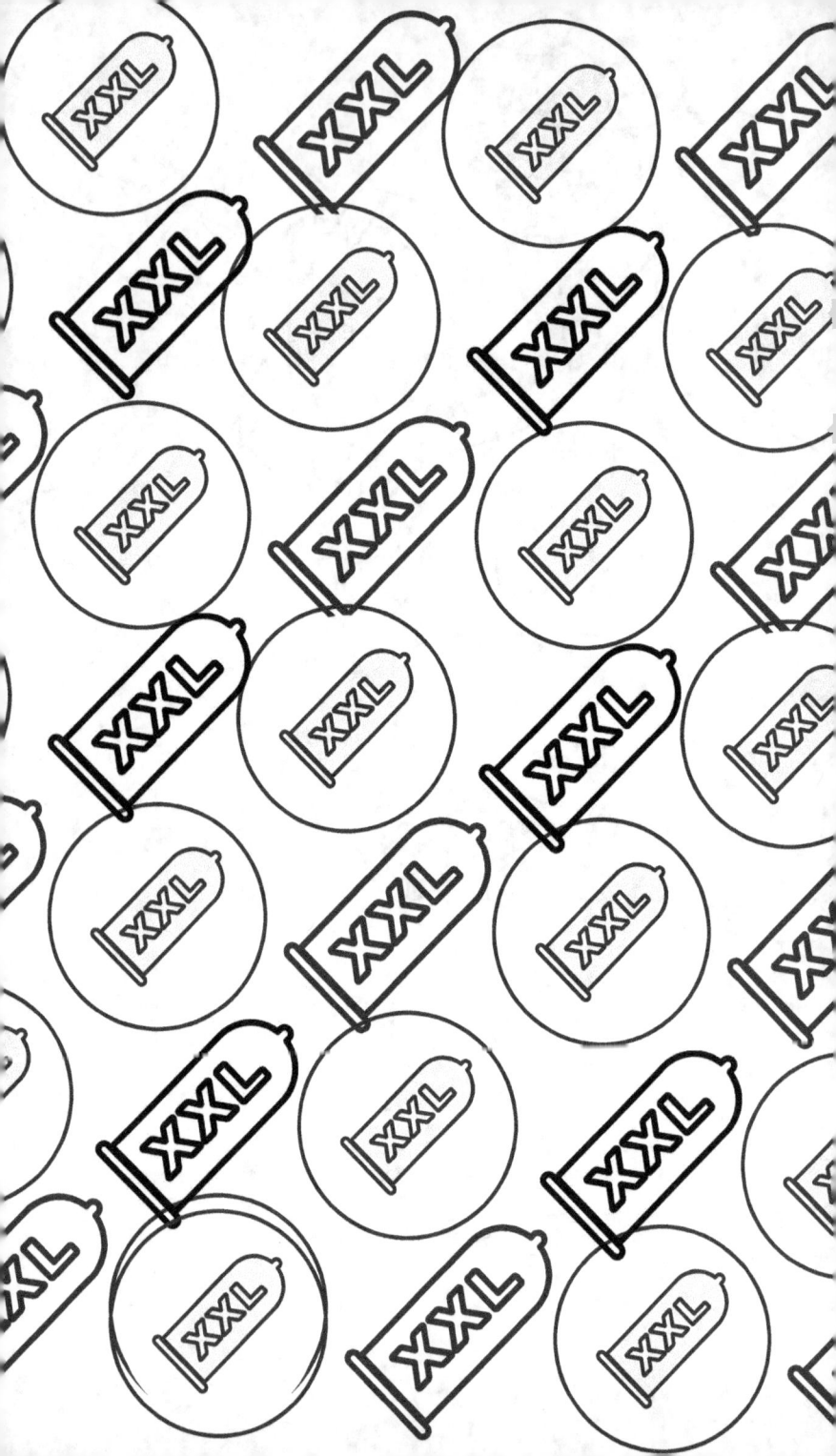

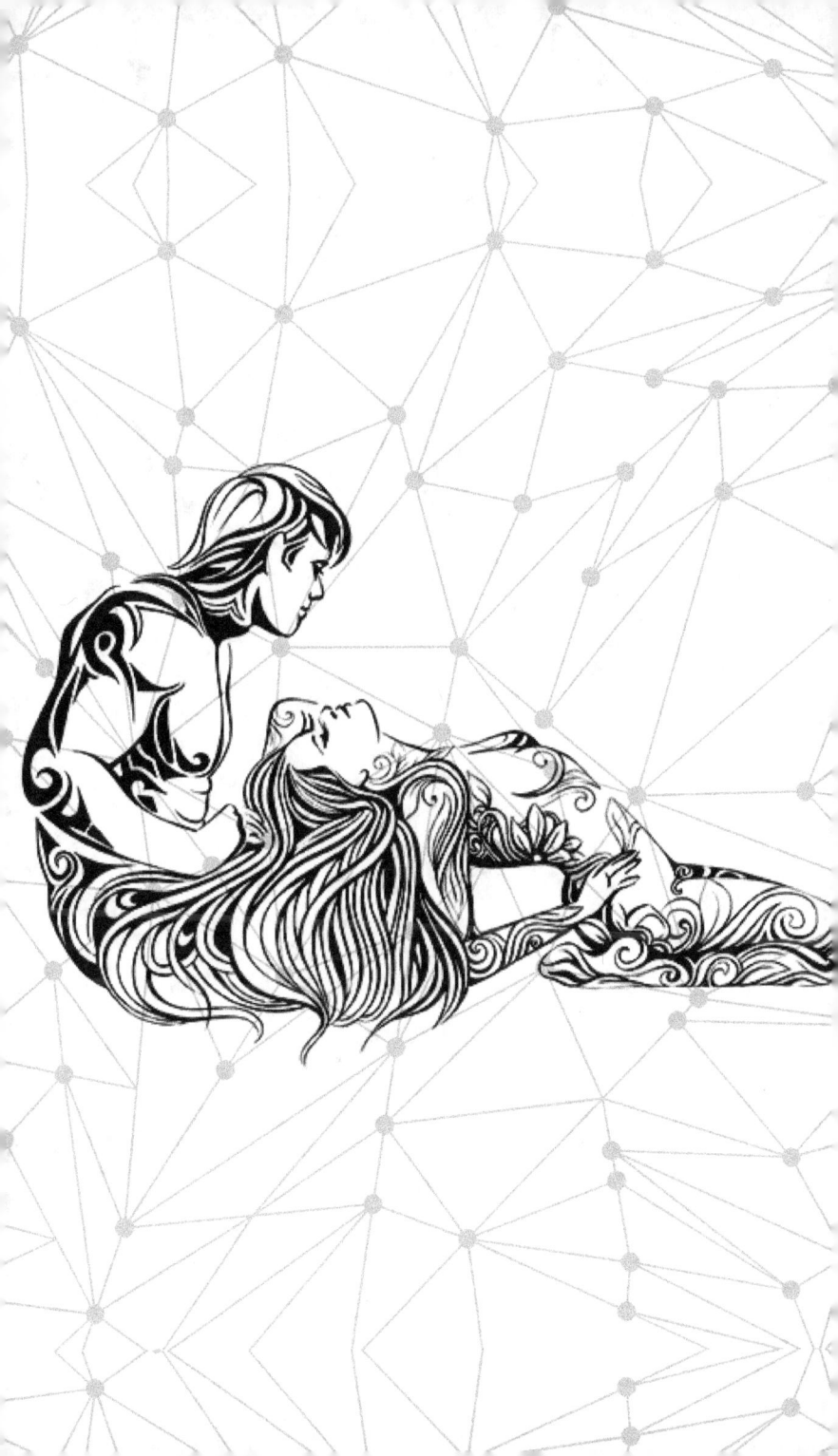

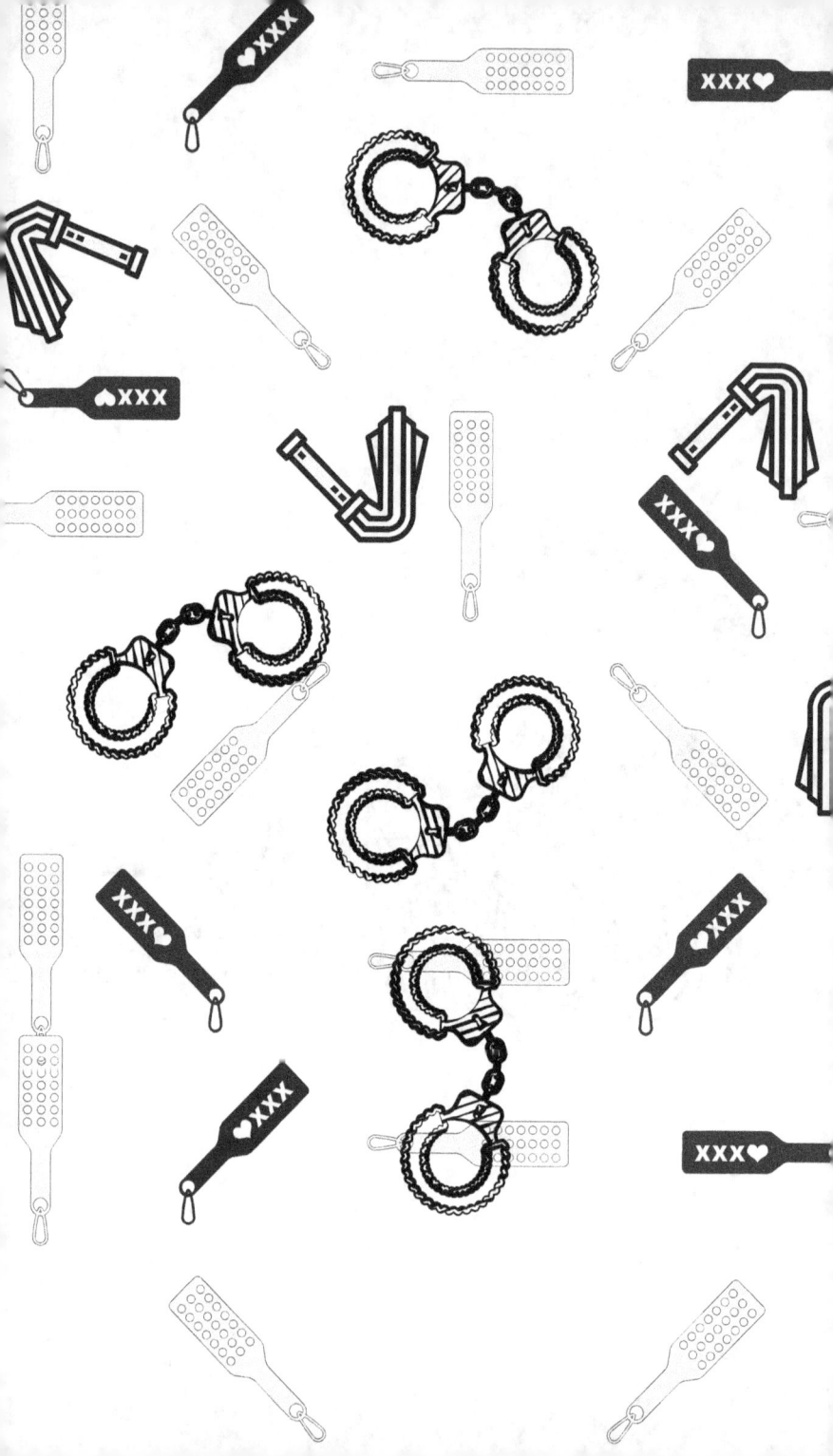

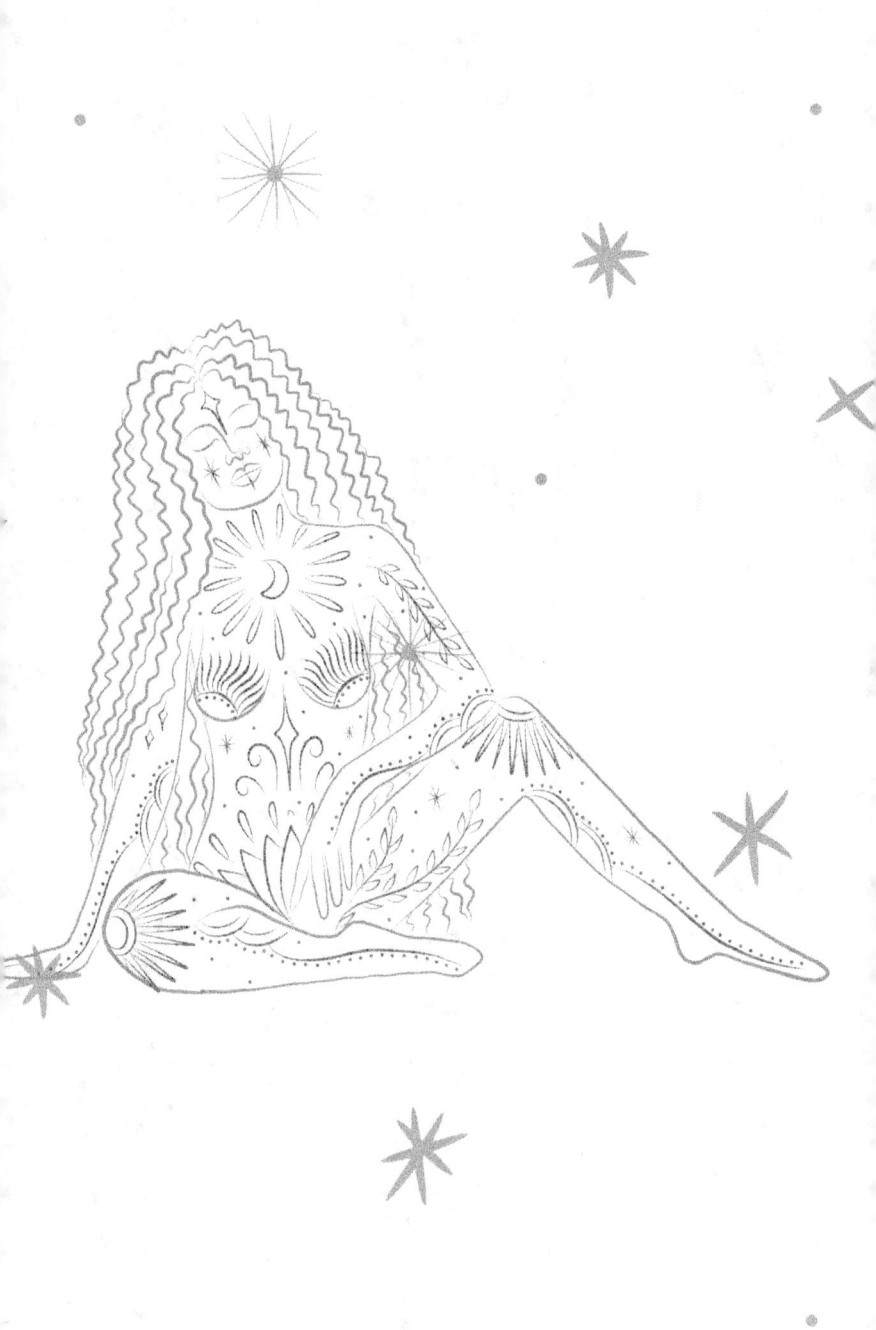

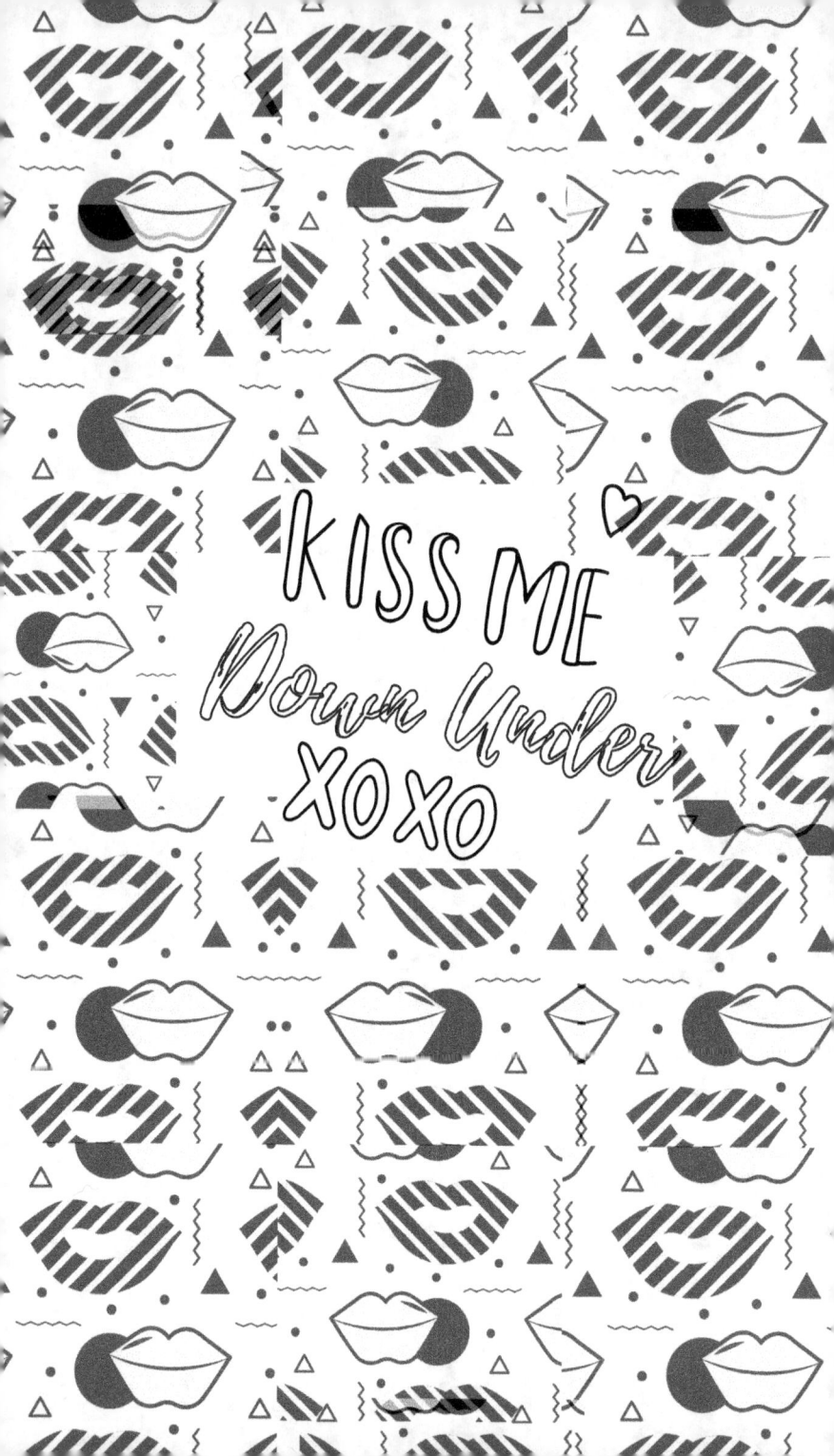

HELLO CLITORIS!

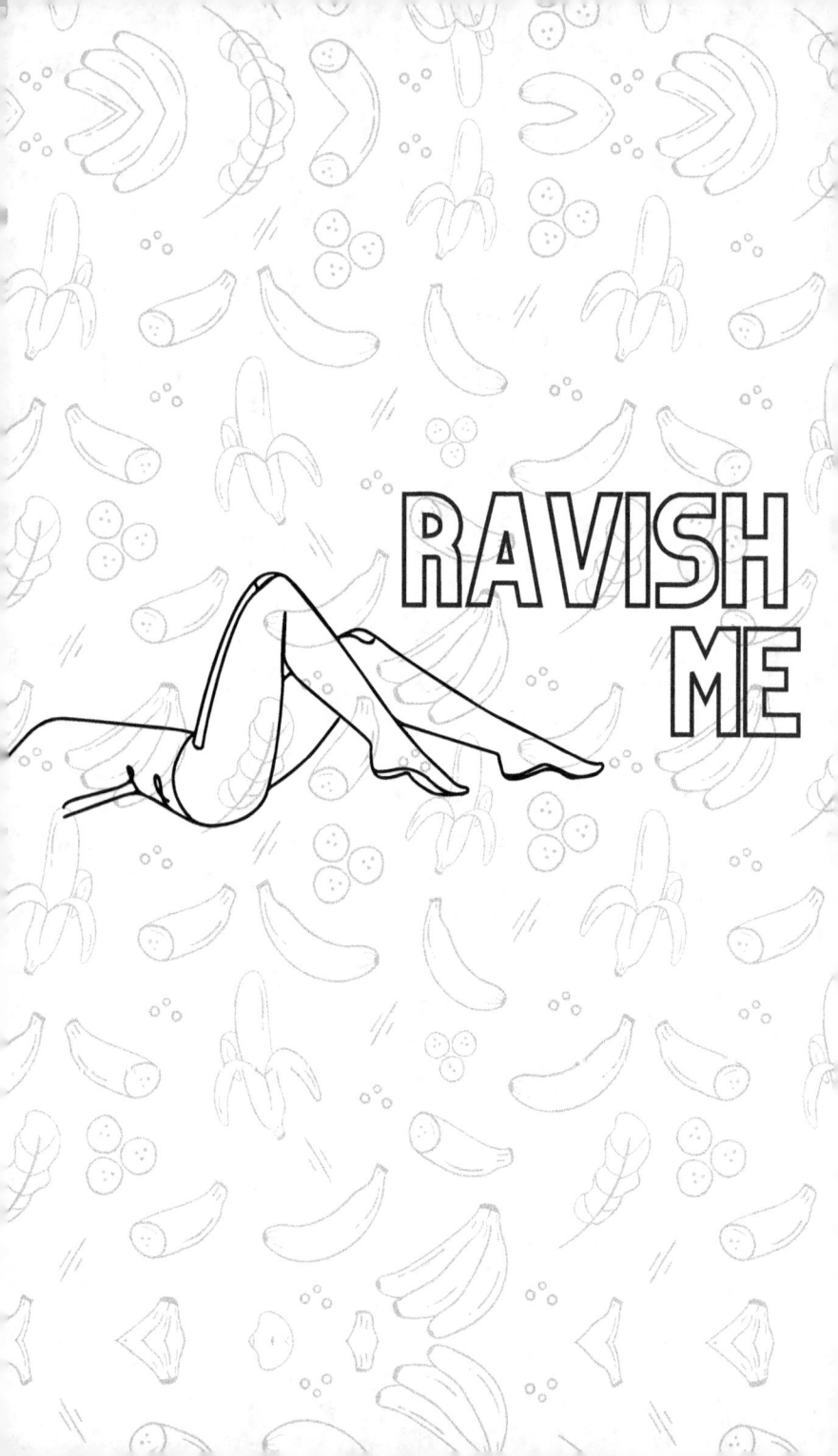

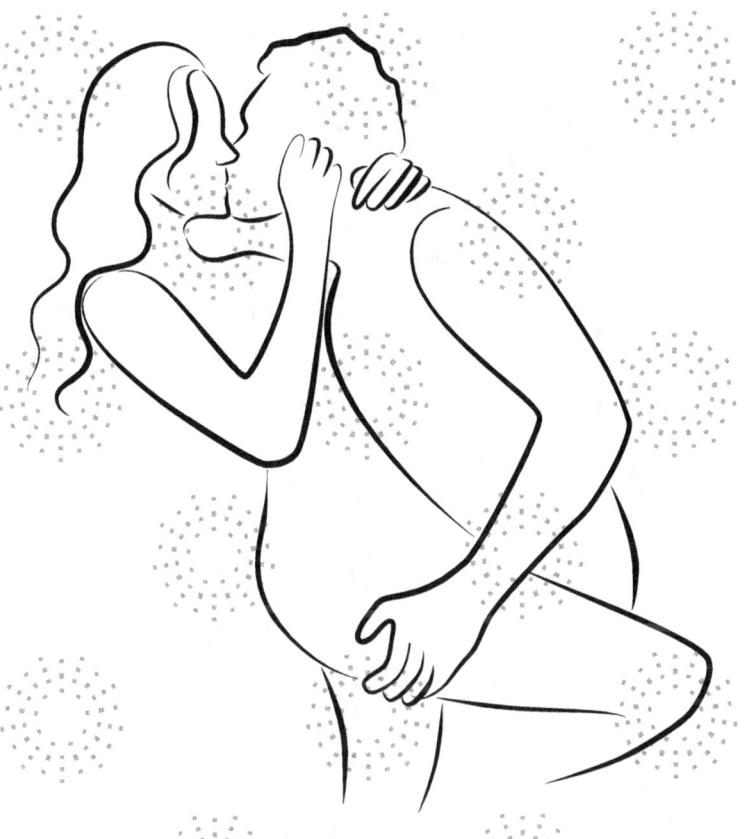

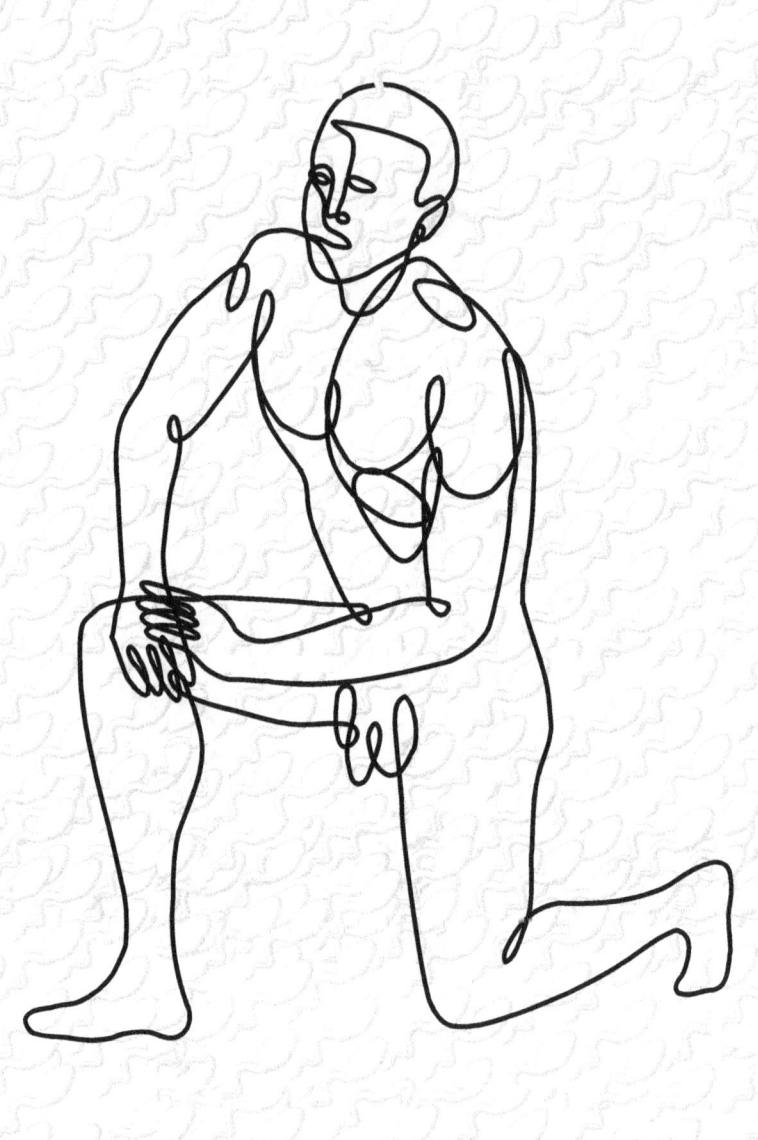

sexy time

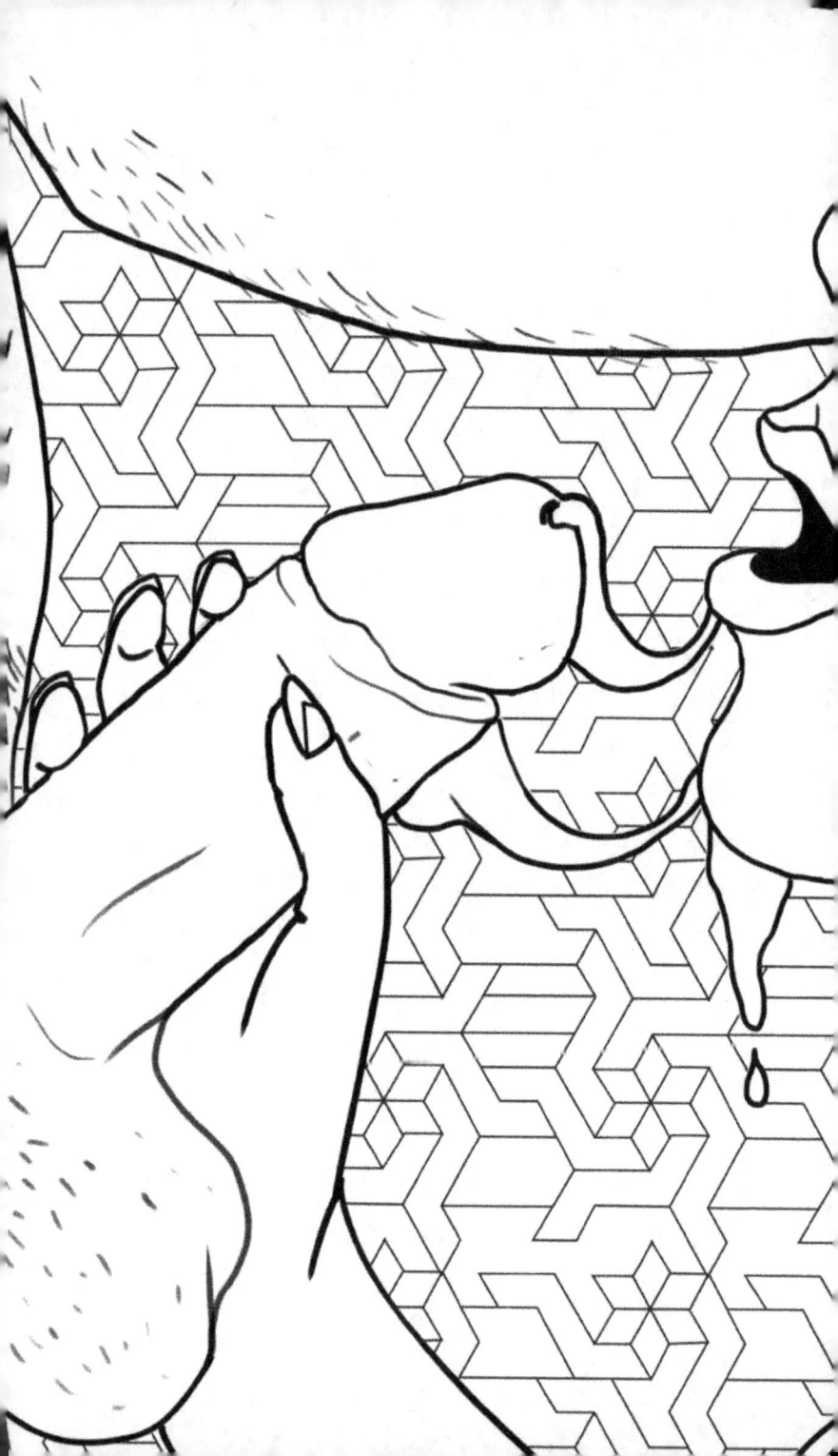

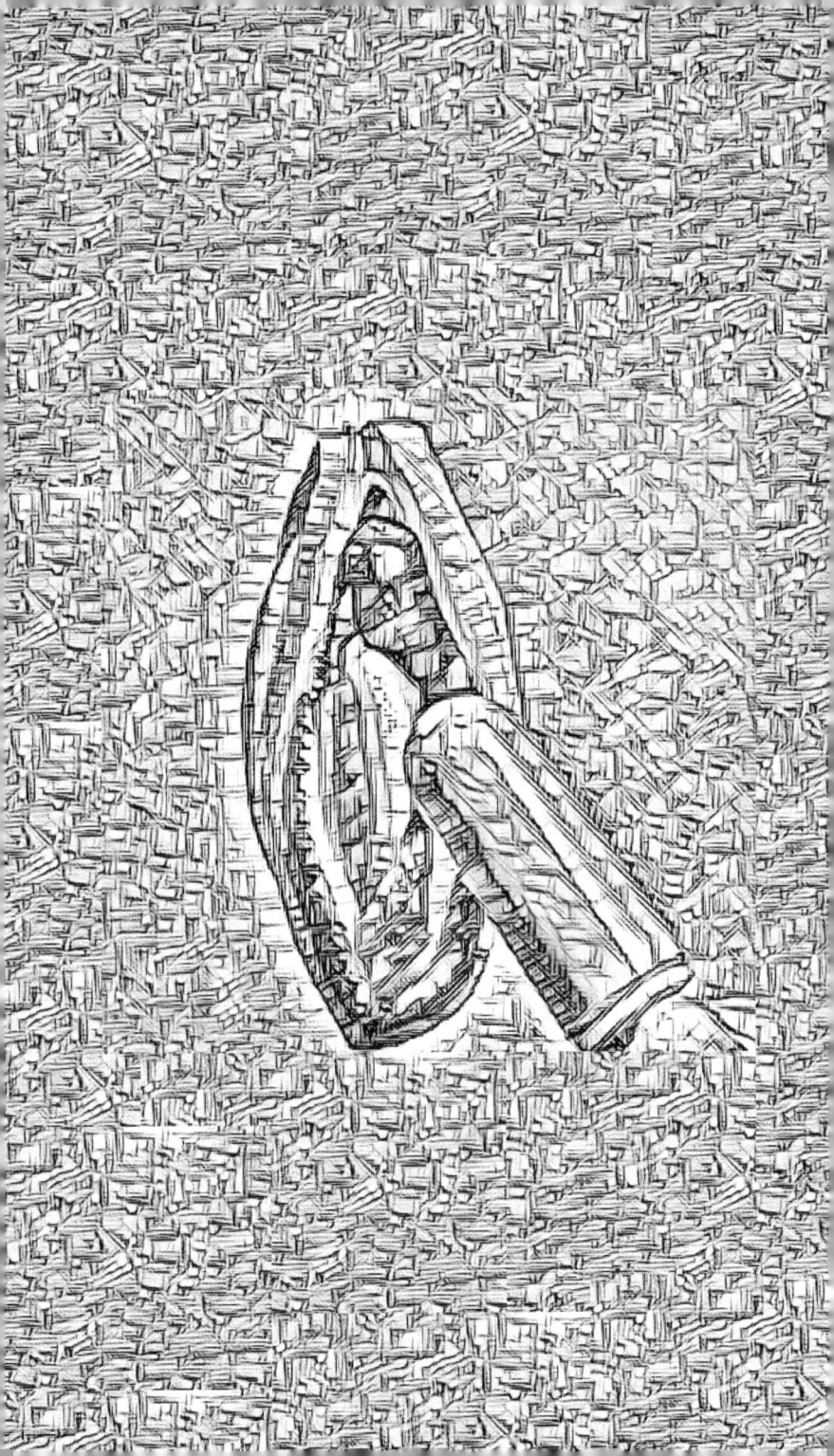

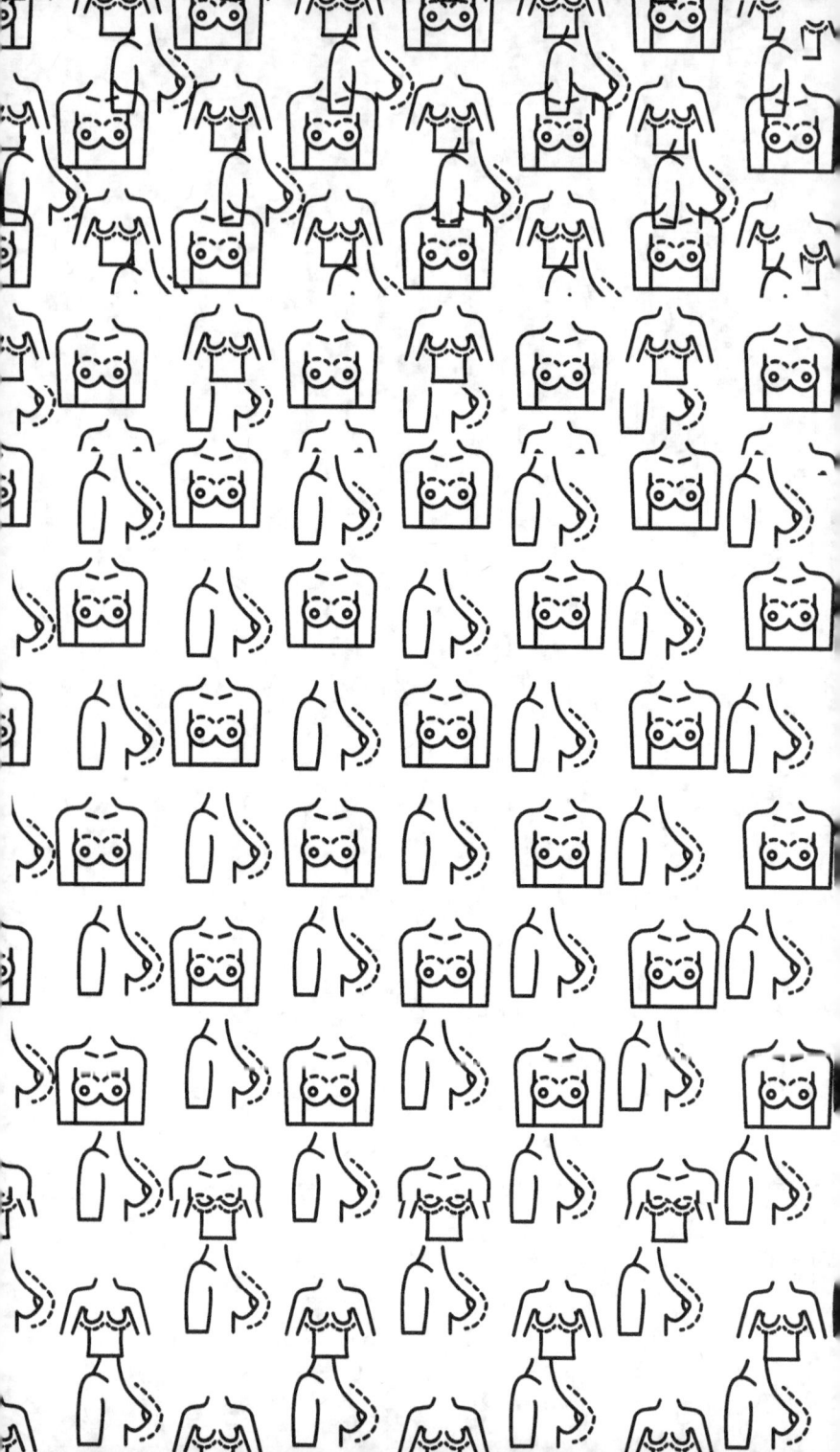

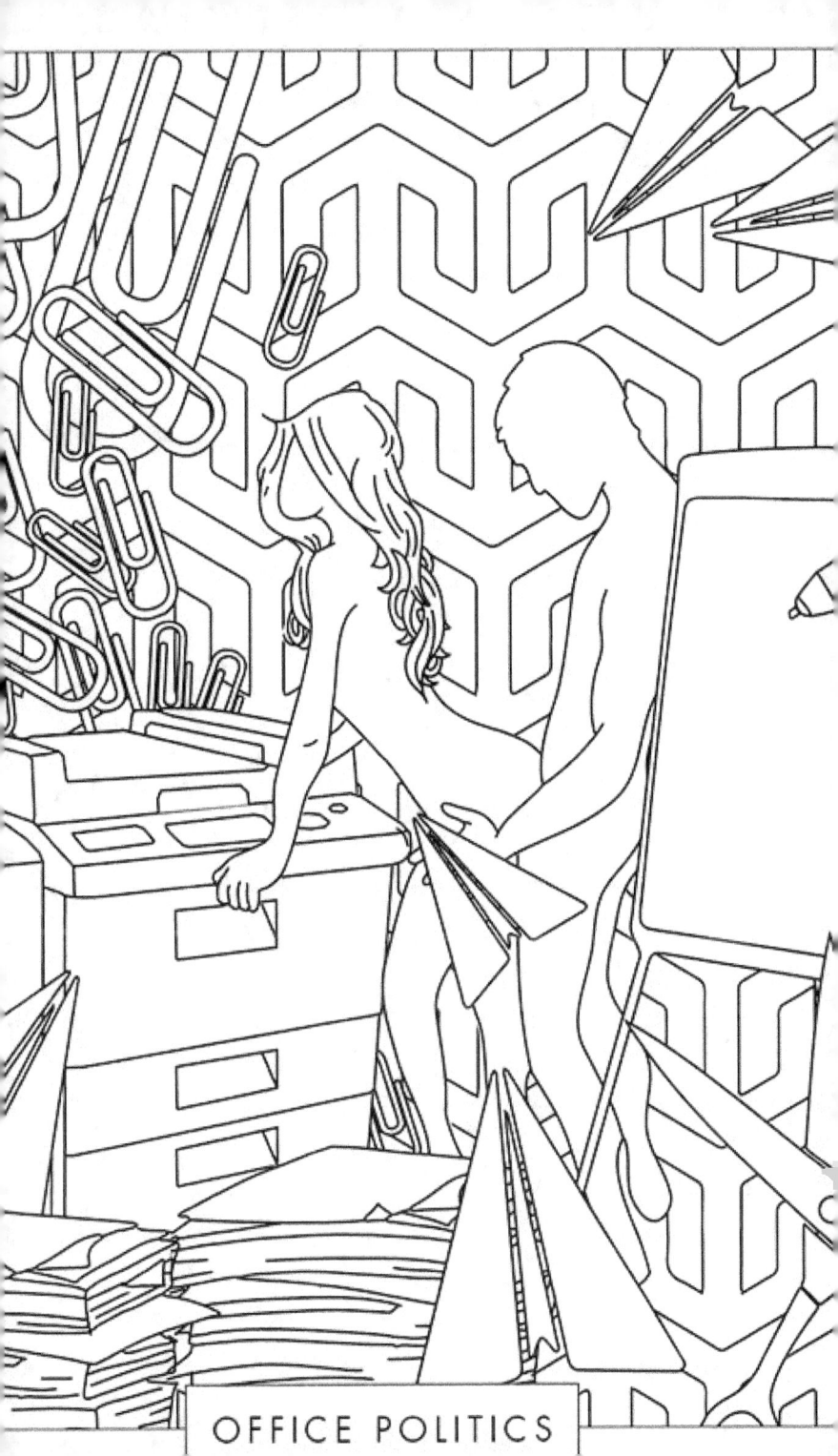

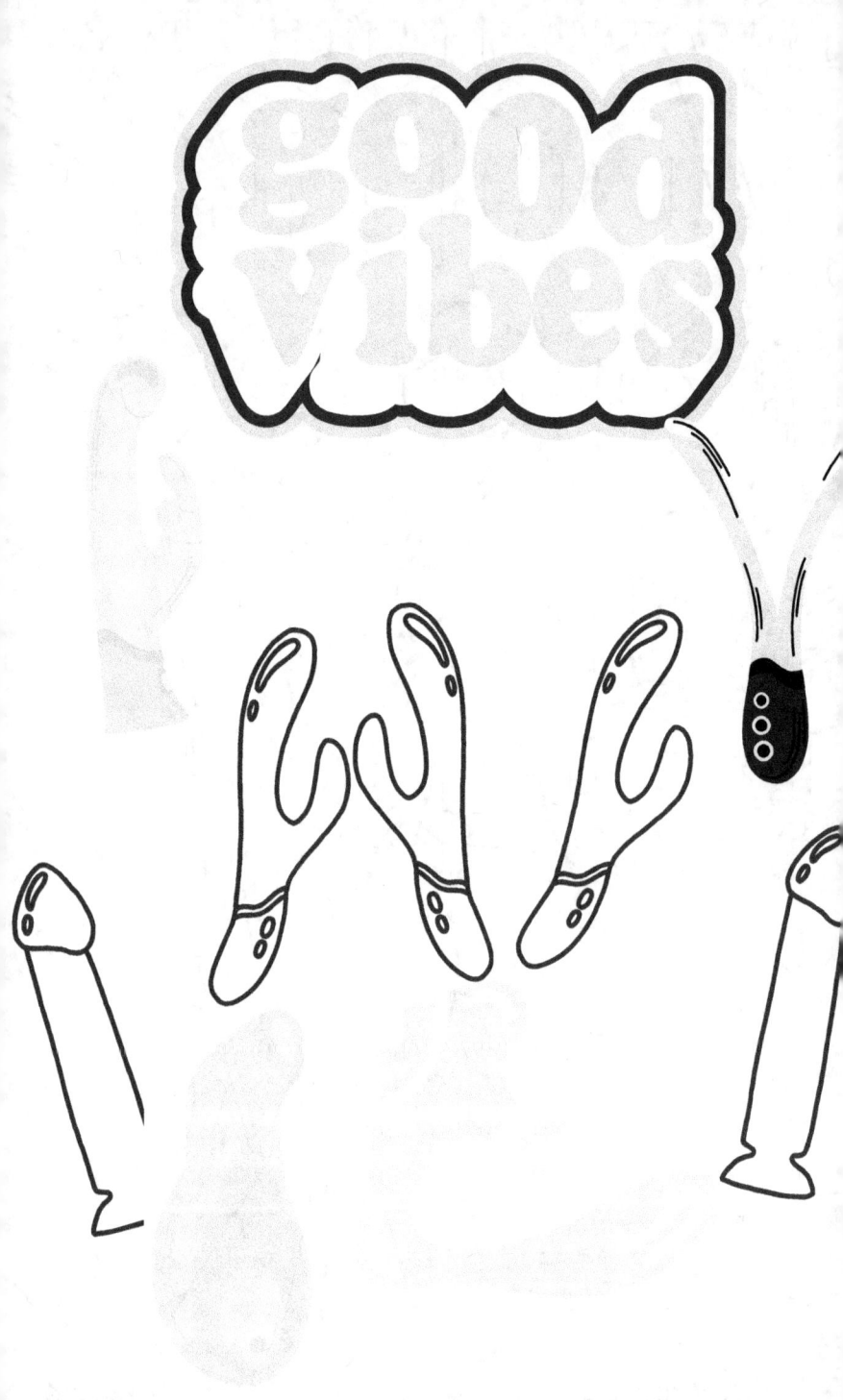

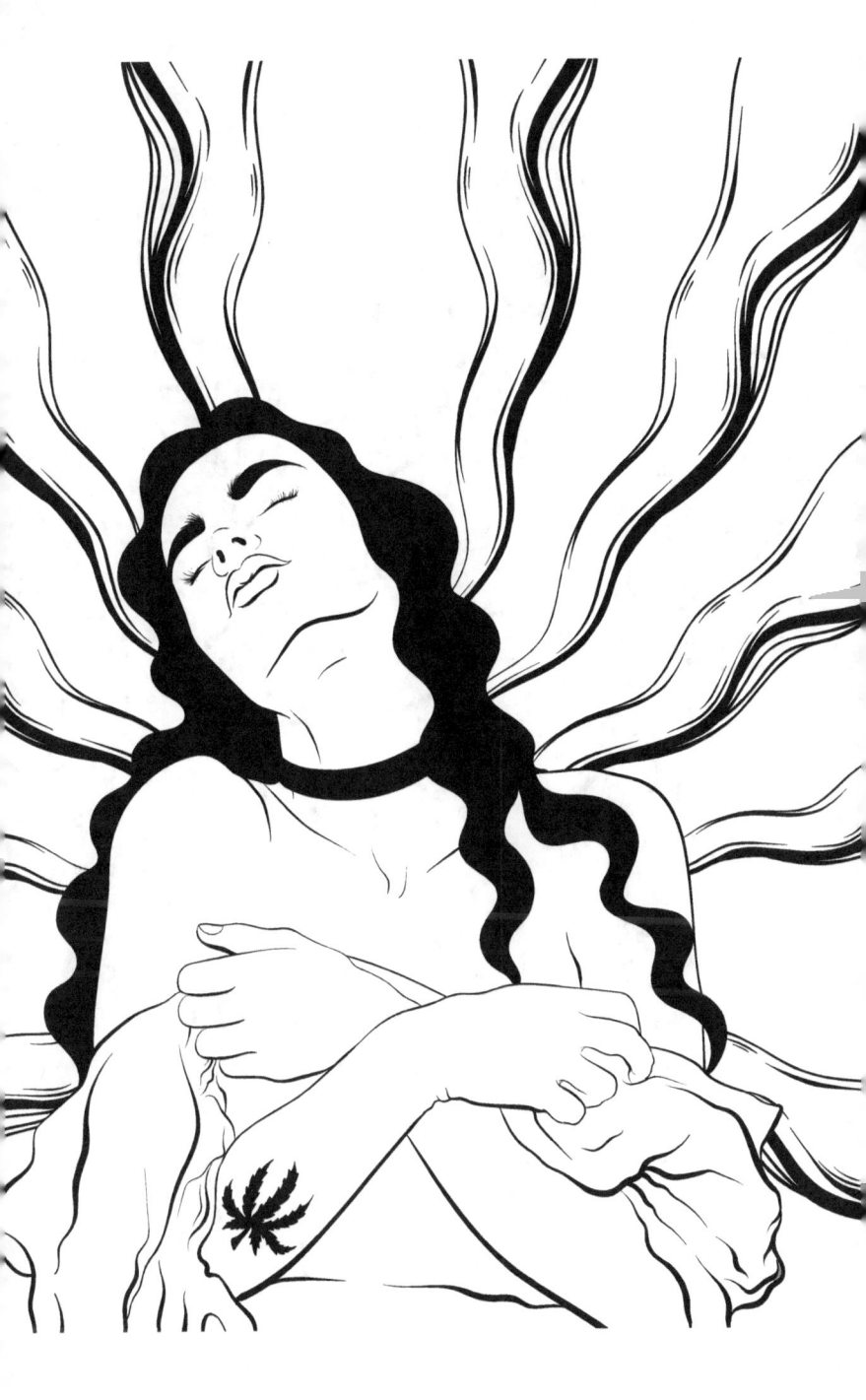

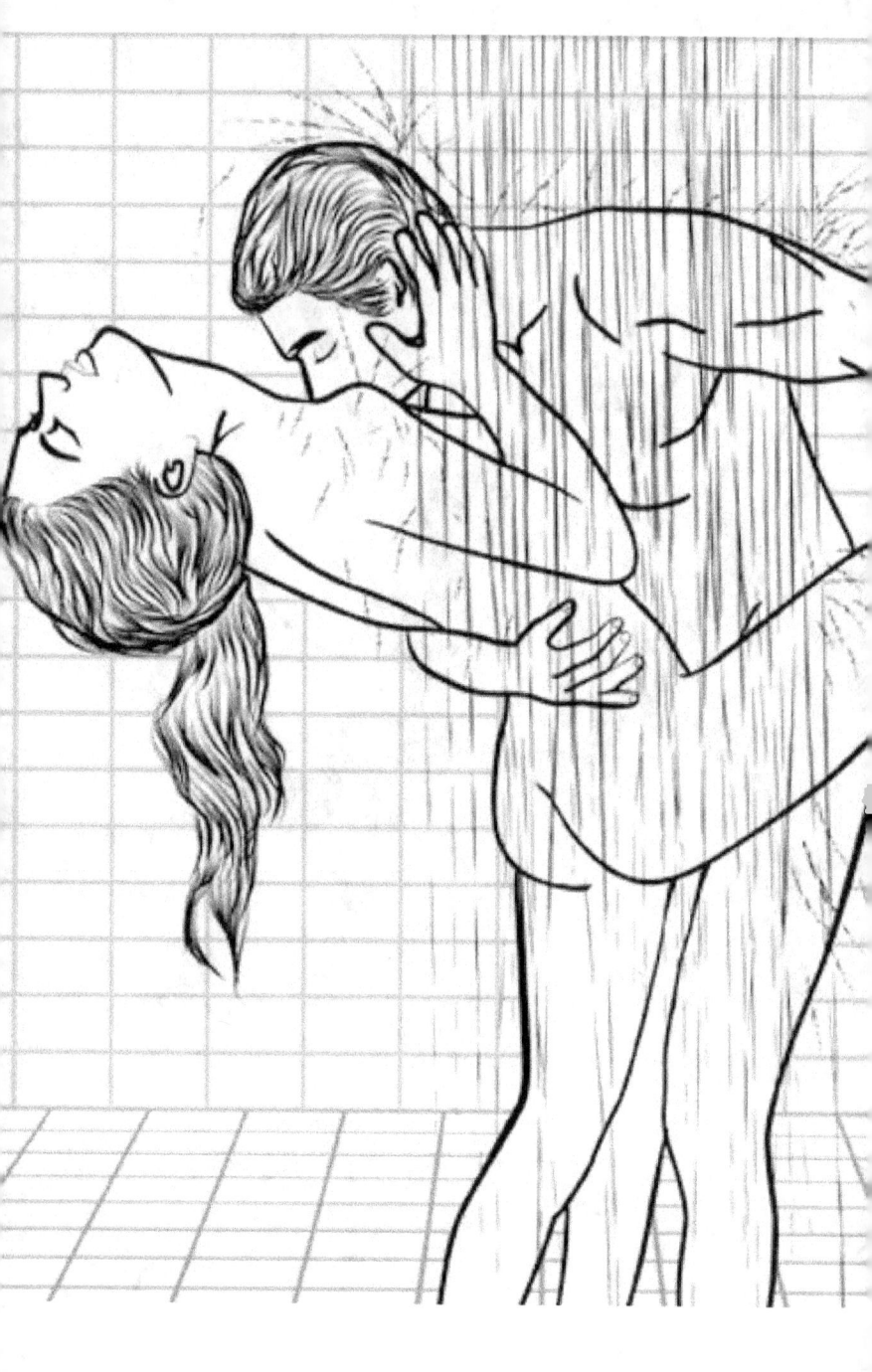

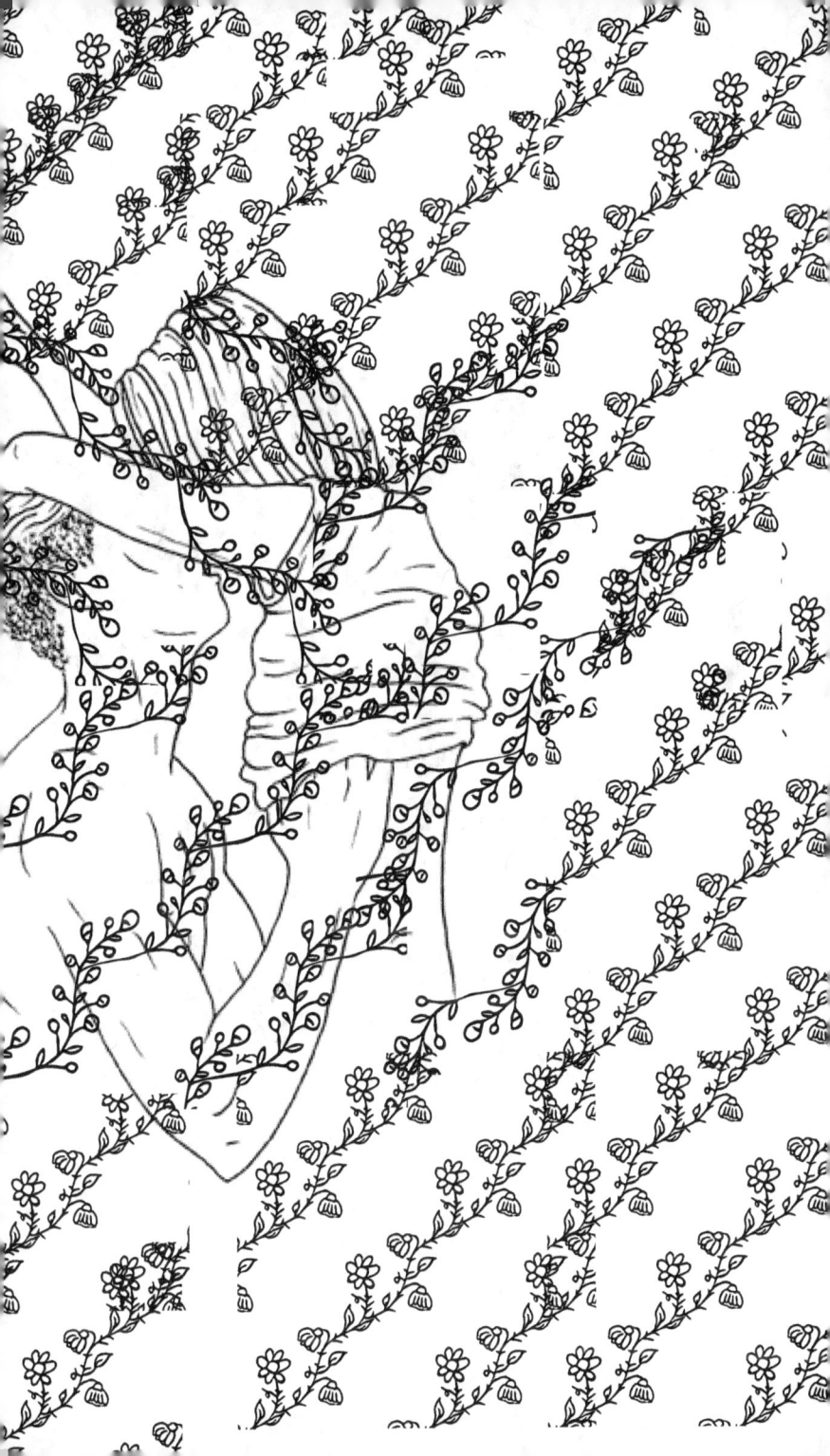

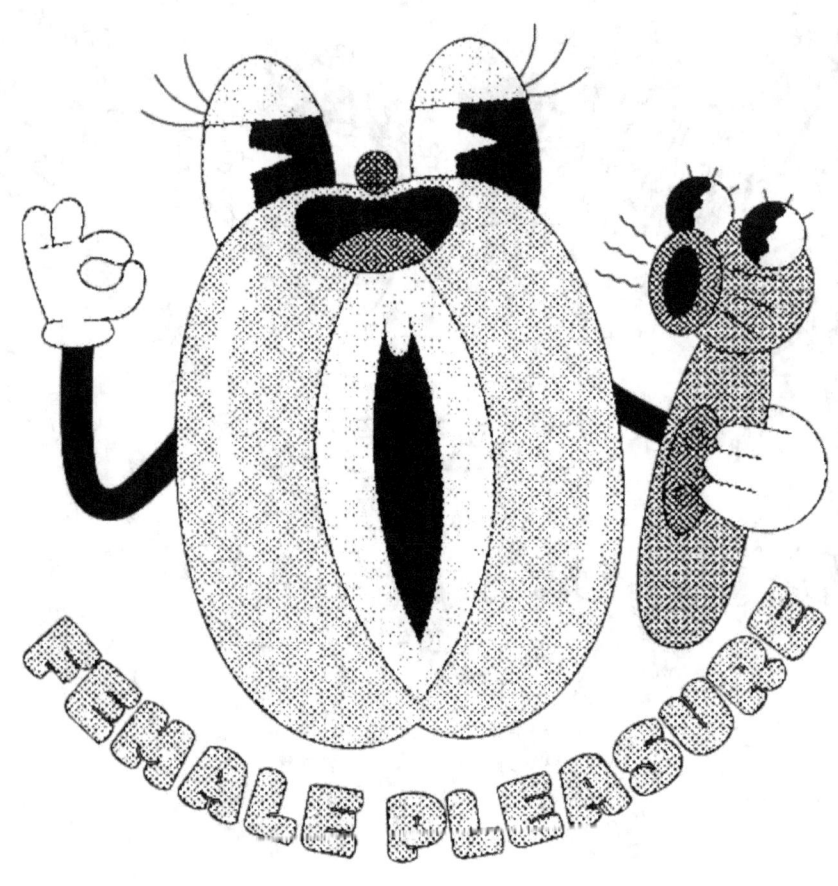

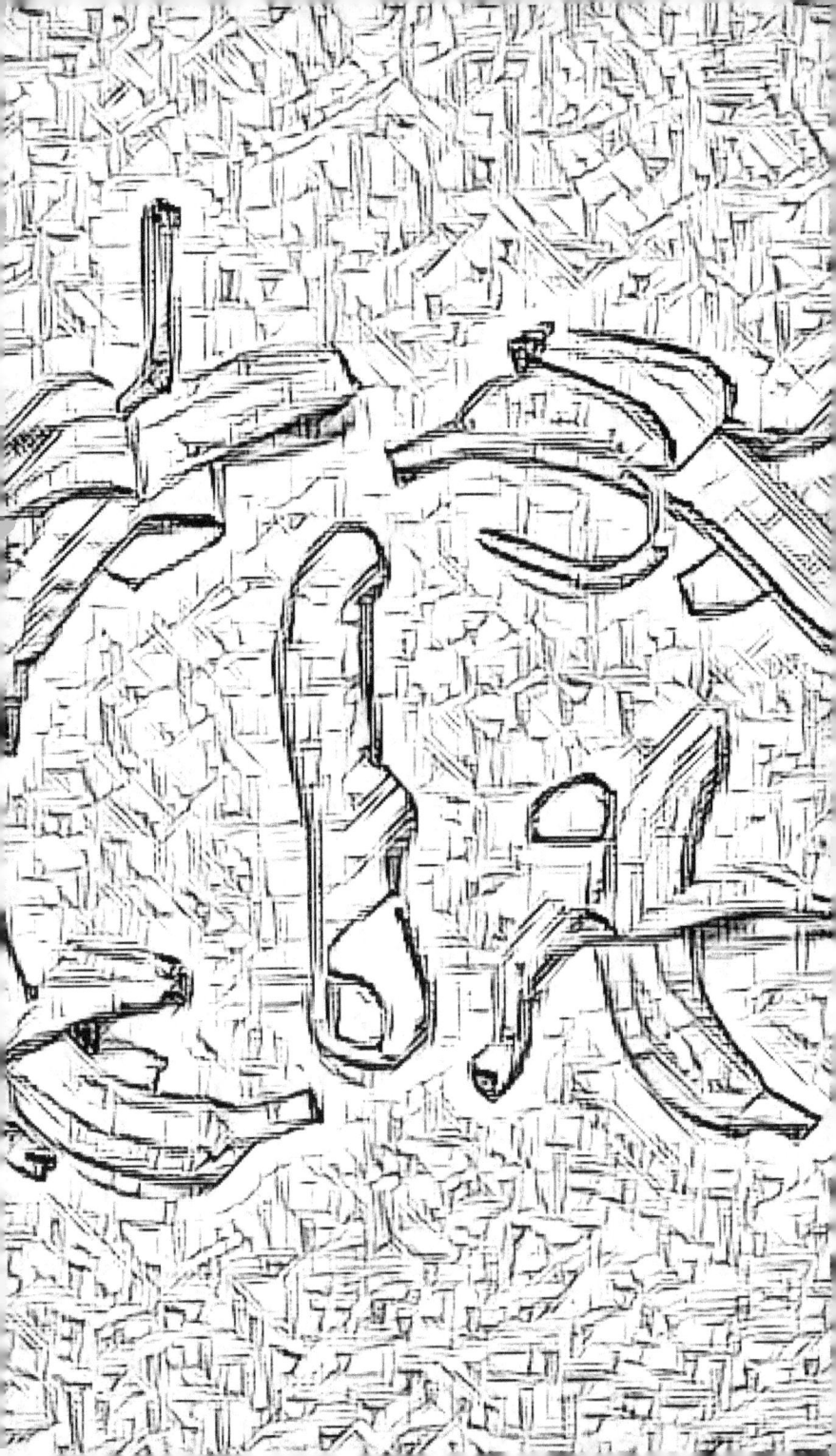

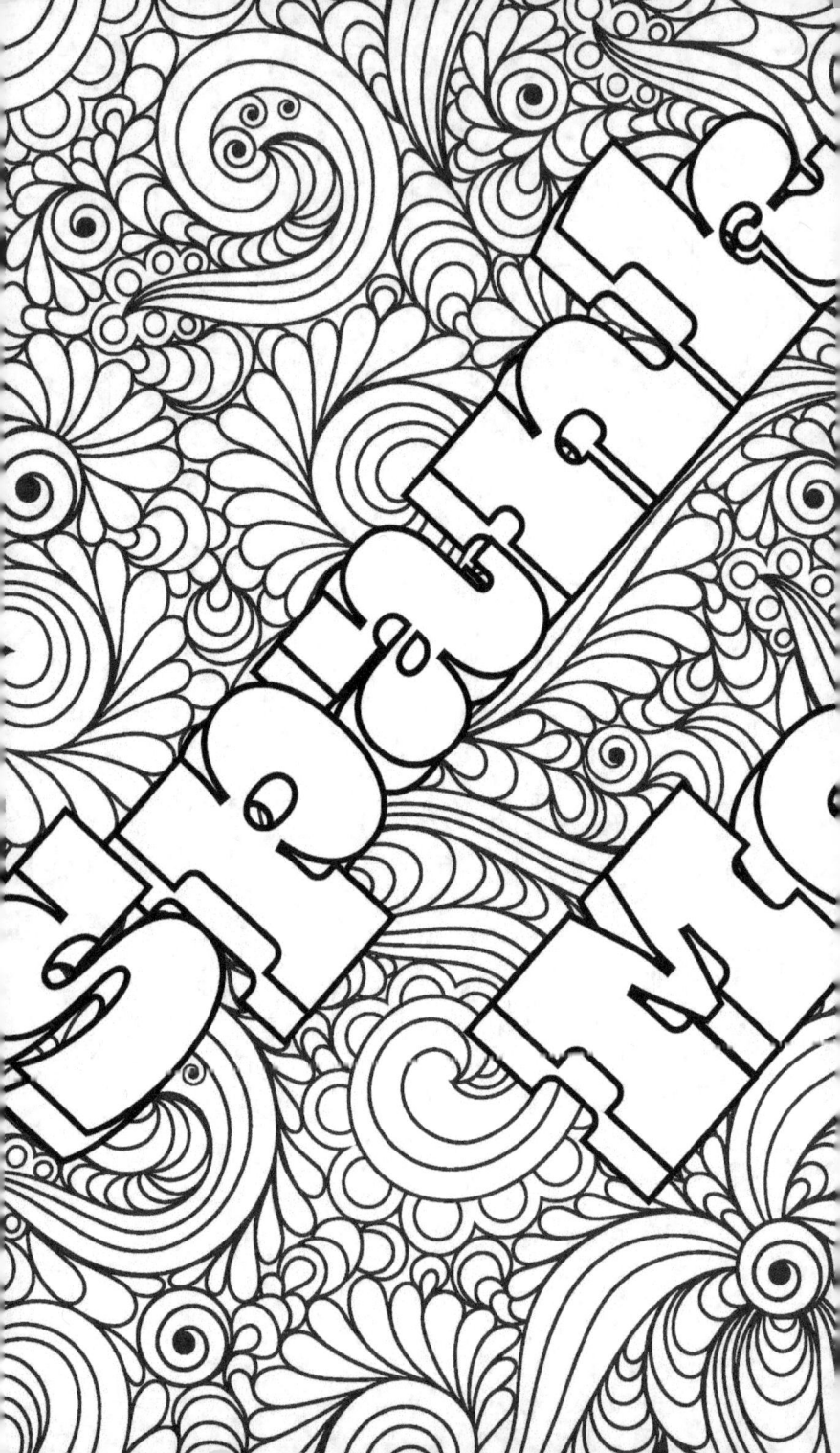

www.ingramcontent.com/pod-product-compliance
Lightning Source LLC
Chambersburg PA
CBHW070322220526
45465CB00013B/2191